Second-Hand Saints

Second-Hand Saints

Illustrated Stories of Christian Spirituality

KEVIN S. REIMER

Illustrations by Ellen V. Rahner

RESOURCE *Publications* · Eugene, Oregon

SECOND-HAND SAINTS
Illustrated Stories of Christian Spirituality

Resource Publications
An Imprint of Wipf and Stock Publishers
199 W. 8th Ave., Suite 3
Eugene, OR 97401

www.wipfandstock.com

PAPERBACK ISBN: 979-8-3852-2839-3
HARDCOVER ISBN: 979-8-3852-2840-9
EBOOK ISBN: 979-8-3852-2841-6

04/01/25

For Monica and Silvio
K.S.R.

For Doug
E.V.R.

Contents

List of Illustrations

Preface

DO YOU REMEMBER LOOKING up to big kids as a grade school student? As children we become aware of personal limitations. We discover our vulnerabilities, sometimes painfully. We learn the world has many problems, some of which are too complicated for eight or nine years of earthly experience. We need someone to emulate, preferably a big kid who has managed to figure out the tough stuff. Therefore, we spent time watching them. We studied their attitudes, behaviors, and habits. We adopted their hairstyles and clothes. We admired their skills and sophistication.

Not much has changed. To be sure, we have grown since the elementary years. Yet the need persists, particularly for Christians living with immediate uncertainties. What does it mean to live faithfully with and through our challenges? The Letter to the Hebrews offers relevant answers. A brilliant overview of faith and perseverance, its punchline is a discourse on the saints—men and women who were faithful to God despite overwhelming, circumstantial impossibilities. By faith they did amazing things, imperfectly. This is what makes them compelling. They are very much like us. Hebrews chronicles the stories of ordinary people who, because of exemplary faith, become participants in the greatest moments of salvation history. They are big kids for grownups.

This book shares the life stories of contemporary Christian faith exemplars. Finding these people wasn't easy. It required collaborators who were committed followers of Christ. Separate meetings were organized for leaders from a faith-based hospice, a nonprofit serving the disabled, a college for teachers, and several church traditions. Leaders were asked a question. How would you identify someone who is an exemplary person of faith? The discussions were impassioned and sometimes contentious. Each group developed a list of criteria or benchmarks for great faith. These criteria were consolidated and returned to the same leaders along with a request. Please identify men and women from your organization or tradition that meet the criteria for faithful exemplarity. Would you kindly provide their contact information?

The interviews took a decade to complete. With one exception, these are everyday people from the pew. You won't recognize them from the media and they are fine with it. All are immersed in service and outreach. Many are involved with peacemaking. Their lives are inspiring. Perhaps surprisingly, they are reluctant—even embarrassed—to hear themselves described as such. It is this unexpected characteristic of faithful exemplarity that is transformative. The spirituality of these remarkable individuals is only self-conscious to the extent that it honors the Triune God of the Universe.

I will share a few observations regarding the stories that follow. First, they are not verbatim accounts. Spoken language is messy. Speakers, even highly articulate individuals, are redundant and sometimes difficult to follow. Speech is frustratingly non-linear. It is peppered with placeholders that can become exhausting to read. The telling of faith exemplar stories required many careful editorial decisions, attempting to balance speaker intent with reader accessibility. The stories in this book are interpretive narratives from faith exemplar interviews, not a collection of transcripts.

Second, the faith exemplars of *Second-Hand Saints* come from American cities. More than anything, this reflects the social networks of collaborating organizations making interview recommendations. Several exemplars are fluent speakers of English as a second language. Some use idioms and grammatical constructions unique to their experiences. I've attempted to honor differences without letting these become a reader distraction. Exemplars tell stories of intimate, personal spiritual experience. Many accounts involve life-changing turning points. Some are excruciatingly painful. Always the editorial effort is to keep the story primary while quietly affirming its origins in particular ethnic and religious contexts.

Finally, faith exemplars in this book reference mentors or historical saints which provide them with comfort and inspiration. These spiritual imprimaturs are a reminder that with each story we are touching a faith legacy that extends back through centuries of church history. Catholic exemplars are particularly and beautifully attentive to this legacy. Christians have at various historical moments experienced vicious persecution, denigration, and cultural shame. A key to the enduring persistence of faith is the example of those who have gone before. The extraordinary illustrations of Ellen Rahner are intended to complement each story for this important reason.

Kevin S. Reimer
Geddes, New York

1

Superhero

I WAS SIX YEARS old. I remember everything clearly. I was in Puerto Rico with my mom. We were walking near the beach and she fell. She was eight months pregnant with my little brother and I helped her up. I remember feeling protective. I was disturbed and anxious when I saw her lying on the ground, very pregnant, bruised, and cut. It took every ounce of strength, but I succeeded in getting her back home. From that day forward I was her *Superman*.

Two years later. My dad abandoned us. There was no trace. We were in the process of moving to New York where there were other Puerto Ricans. I distinctly remember leaving. I will never forget the smell of the school. I loved that smell. It smelled like a newly sharpened pencil, the smell of an old Catholic school. There was distant choral music that sounded like St. Peter's gate. It was the last day of school and I was leaving. My teacher gave me a little gift. I didn't know what was waiting for me when I got to New York. But I felt safe and happy and I was excited because I was flying on a plane with my mom and brother. It was the last memory I have of feeling secure and safe.

Two decades later. My little brother was coming home from work in the Bronx. Someone drove past him, pulled out a gun, and shot him dead. My little brother was twenty-three years old. There was no motivation, no altercation. My brother wasn't into drugs or gangs. He wasn't doing anything like that. He was working as a substitute teacher and he was coming home from an elementary school. They shot him on the sidewalk and he died and my life changed. There was a special bond between us. I was the super-hero. He called me *Batman*. Of course, he was Robin.

My brother was a talented musician who had joined a band. They were on the verge of getting a recording contract. I had to watch my mother's agony, watch her suffering. It changed us forever and it happened for no reason. It was a random act, and it shook me to the very core. I didn't know if I could continue to believe in God. I didn't know how to make sense of it. I felt devastated, like my insides had been hollowed out. I felt abandoned. He was the baby of the family. He was adorable and cute and funny, this gentle spirit. It turned out the shooter was an eighth-grade kid. The entire thing was a living nightmare.

How could God let this happen? How could a middle school kid have evil intent to do something like this? I started thinking about God's will. If this is God's will, then I hate God. I talked to my priest and began studying the bible. No answers. More frustration. I went to counseling. That brought up abandonment issues with my father. It became exponential anger, more anger than I could manage. I was angry with God and I was angry with society and I was angry with the kid's parents. I was angry with the system. I began to lose faith in the rule of law. There was no justice here, just hopelessness. I was upset, hurt, disillusioned with God.

At first it was numbness. Then it was pain. After a long time it became faith. My faith became a huge piece of it. I would go to Mass and sit in the communion of saints. I would receive the Eucharist and think, *I'm on this side of the table and my brother is on the other side with all those that have gone before.* I couldn't do much, so I prayed. Most of the time I didn't have words. My prayers were tears. To cope, I began to write out prayers and memorize them. I would go to church and say those memorized prayers, along with the readings. Saying prayers with the community, that really helped me. It gave me hope, all of us together praying these ancient prayers. For two thousand years these prayers have been chanted and sung and spoken in unison by Christian communities. Present, past, and future came together in those sacred moments. For me, experiencing such deep loss and confusion and sorrow in a community became the difference. Being there. Being on this side of the table. That became the focal point for me.

In the middle of this I visited my grandmother. She was a Pentecostal minister and a former missionary. She said something I will never forget. "You can get angry with God, and he can take it."

A huge weight came off my shoulders. I went back to school to become an attorney. I was able to overcome my brother's murder. The tragedy wasn't able to defer everything in my life. It was a gift to overcome such evil and find my footing, to be strong and courageous and do what I thought needed to be done. I was able to

3

get back on track and move in a new direction. Evil wasn't going to overcome my life or decisions.

It took time, needing to calm down and take a deep breath. Getting past the hate, that kid must be punished, you know. All of these things. My faith is scripture, trusting in wisdom beyond my understanding, standing on this side of the table. Standing with the community reminds me that my experience is not unusual. Others before me have known this kind of pain. That's what helped me because there's no human way to understand and accept it. Turning to God and scriptures and reading the stories of the exile and how the Israelites were called to God. Delivered by God. Not that I understand everything but trusting in the fact that I come from a tradition, a legacy of God's faithfulness.

2

Epitemia

I WAS A TEACHER, once upon a time. You teach because you think it makes a difference. You teach because teachers are people everyone seems to remember as yogi. The one who changed my life. The teacher is that special person who saw my potential. Does magic happen because the person is a teacher? Or is it desperation for trusted relationships? In America news is entertainment and phones collect our data. Celebrities are gods and people don't speak with their neighbors. You become a teacher because you want to be a guru. All you are doing is stealing those window paper dolls of teachers and students on display for Back-to-School Night. You are stealing them and pressing them into the vacant recesses of your heart. You are using them to fill the void.

I spent the last year of my teaching career in depression. It was killing me. The kids were driving me crazy. It was changing me into something I loathed. I was becoming an unhappy person. An antisocial person. I had no experience with depression. It made things terribly difficult at school. I left and went to Scotland. On spring break of my last teaching year, I went to visit a friend on the west coast, an isolated and remote part of the country. It was a windswept little island with a famous abbey and turquoise water that looked like the Bahamas. The locals said the population of sheep was five times the number of humans. My friend hosted me for three weeks. I lived on her couch. It was like the feeling of aloe on a bad sunburn. Have you ever experienced that? Deeply cooling, soothing. It was the first hint that I might be healed from the things that were making me depressed. I tried not to burden my friend. I didn't talk much about myself or my feelings. But when she put me on the boat to go home it was clear she knew just how deeply I was hurting. "I know this is really hard for you, please come back anytime. Let me know. Come."

I was floored. Here was a friend inviting me to stay with her like someone would invite a sibling or cousin with cancer. Good heavens, what an invitation! I already knew my teaching career was over. It was scary as hell, but I pulled the ripcord and bailed out. I had been reading about simple living. I took advantage of the moment to sell much of what I owned. It was liberation. It made me feel like it was OK to take her up on the incredible offer. Back to Scotland I went. Three months later I was on the same little ferry, headed to her island at the end of the world. The boat was heaving up and down on big green waves from the North Atlantic. Huge rollers that began in places like Greenland and Iceland. With each heave I realized how sick I was. Broken, retching. It was the first time in my life I had experienced anything like that. I was always the person who had it together, who rode the wave and made it bend to my will. Now the waves were crashing down on me. Cue maudlin thoughts, dramatic thunderclaps. I am drowning.

I didn't want people to see me like this. Strangers, friends, it didn't matter. I was so consumed that I hid from the ferry employee who was responsible for getting cars off the boat. I curled up in the trunk and hid. "Don't worry, just come." I kept holding onto her words. They were like a lifeline. I could see her face, hear her voice. "We will be together, no expectations. We will cook and we will walk." She was working at the island abbey, part of a community which was rebuilding it. She was the first person in my entire life who didn't need to receive something back from me. I mean, think about it. Even your parents need something from you, something that makes their trouble worthwhile, a story they can boast about with their friends. Payback for mom's meatloaf. My friend didn't need any of that. She really, truly, honestly wanted me to come and stay. When she said it was no trouble, she meant it. Just bring yourself, wherever you are, however you are. Let's be together. When you boil it down, isn't that what life is about? I now understand her invitation as the pearl of great price.

It was a turning point for me. Over six months I slowly healed. I was praying one morning in the abbey. There were Celtic high crosses in the yard and chapel. Really, really old. Dating back to a time before the Middle Ages, to St. Columba. The crosses were speaking to me. They were reminding me. God was doing this profound work and it happened in a very mundane way. My friend was a good cook and a vegetarian and I was healed through food. I was healed by stacking firewood and picking up driftwood on the beach. I was healed by getting hay for the sheep. I was healed by reading. I previously had this idea that God heals in an instant, like when Jesus put his hands on someone who was sick. I am sure it came from my mother's church background. But there was never anyone talking about what was happening to me in Scotland, that someone might love me for who I am, not because I've worked my butt off to make them happy. Simple, mundane life. Walking, reading, being with people and moving away. Back home everyone was commuting, entertaining, busy busy busy. Here there wasn't anything to do except what nature gives you.

I was walking the island shore on a windy day, thinking about gravity and God. That's me. If it wasn't already hard enough to walk through dry sand while depressed, I'll double down and make things harder. I was reading some crazy stuff about M-theory, a way of understanding gravity. I won't bore you with the details, except to say that gravity might involve probability that is weirdly predictable from the beginning—it starts with a prior assumption. This assumption allows for things to happen randomly, but within limits established by that assumption. Confused? To me it seemed like a kind of purpose. Or what is purposeful. The chaos is managed and directed by purposeful order. While I was walking the beach, my world felt random and chaotic. The wind was blowing my life circumstances around, swirling and buffeting me. But it wasn't completely random. The wind, dry sand, and my tired feet were all subject to gravity, pulling with tiny strings of even tinier particles. I don't think God is the gravity, but God orchestrates it. We are pulled in a purposeful way toward a paradox in space and time. I invented a name for it. I called it the *already and not yet paradox*. Here I am struggling with depression, grief, plenty of busted stuff. My suffering is being healed in space and time, already and not yet realized. God is revealed in the same way, already and not yet. The prior assumption is that God heals. The prior assumption puts a boundary around what seems disordered, pulling us toward something not fully realized.

I knew that God could heal me. I believed it as a kid and I believe it now. It's not a Netflix show starring Jesus. It has nothing to do with our worthiness. It might be very slow, even painfully slow. I am from the East Bay. My mom came from an evangelical church. She was emotional and very expressive. My dad was the opposite. He was formal and distant. My parents did their best, they gave me what they knew. But now I was experiencing something different. The wind was howling off the ocean and I was up to my shins in the sand. Each step was an effort. I was pulling my foot out of the suction with nothing to support the next step. Isn't that depression in a nutshell? Yet gravity never let me go. It was there, giving me something I could count on, secure and predictable. I kept moving forward and sand began to disappear, gradually replaced by the smooth rock of the island. Ancient rocks, from the basement of space and time. My steps became easier. I finally had something underneath, something to push off. The wind wouldn't quit but things felt solid. Grounded. The prior assumption is that God heals. The long walk on the beach became an allegorical story, where I could work out depression and experience God's touch.

I walked and my thoughts kept going back to the high crosses at the abbey. I decided to move in that direction. At that moment it hit me. I was on a pilgrimage that was purposefully directed away from depression and toward the healing touch of God. Later when I told my friend, she got excited. She called it a pilgrimage of penance. At first, I was confused. I had weird ideas that penance was about self-punishment in places like the Philippines. People beating themselves. But this was different. She told me about *epitemia,* the ancient idea that penance–admission of my weaknesses, failings, imperfections–had purpose. Epitemia was a golden opportunity for God's reconciliation. For healing. The depression wasn't a broken finger or paper cut. It was bigger. More serious. It was my self-loathing, a sense of myself as worthless, and the ways I had hurt others with those things. It was a large green wave headed toward me, a rogue wave, traveling miles across the Atlantic to capsize my life and send me to the bottom. Epitemia was the purpose, the gravitational pull on my life. It was a force moving me toward reconciliation and healing that is already and not yet. A special reminder that God is engaged and concerned with everything in the universe.

Skip ahead one year. I went to visit a friend at her parents' house in Gallup, New Mexico. My friend is a full Navajo. We have a very frank and honest relationship, the kind where you can talk about anything even if we don't always see eye-to-eye. It comes from a deep appreciation of who she is and where she's been. Where she comes from. We were hiking in the canyonlands. She has a deep spirituality. It's wisdom and ritual and community all rolled together. Ancestors and history. It's spirituality that comes from a tradition going all the way back to the foggy dawn of humanity. She began telling amazing stories about each mesa, plant, and animal. She explained that God was inside each of these, but not the same as them. Each held sacred value for her people. Together, they provided symbols and food and inspiration to generations of Navajo. They were actors in the stories elders would tell the younger generation. While we walked, she applied the same ideas to my depression and the Scottish beach. It was attractive but it didn't fully resonate. I wasn't healed by spiritual energies connected to animate and inanimate objects. I wasn't healed by a confederation of deities. I was healed by a very particular Other. I was sure of it. It was God who existed in a coherent, identifiable sense. This God had total, creative latitude with every animate and inanimate object, intimate knowledge of each as creator. Working through the already and not yet paradox, God was active, not merely present. Jesus already. Jesus not yet. Me—in process, under construction, but headed in a purposeful direction because of the Holy Spirit. Ready for another paradox? Even if I didn't agree with her idea of God, it made complete sense to me. My take was a twist on her spiritual ideas. The sand and wind on that Scottish beach weren't reminders of God in the sense of giving concrete evidence of the divine. They were reminders that God wasn't done with me. I'm known by an Other, interested in stuff like reconciliation and healing. This Other is really, really big.

I laugh now. I live on a houseboat named *Epitemia*. I am not joking. It's probably the first boat named penance in any language. The houseboat is made from concrete and somehow doesn't sink despite the pull of quantum particle strings. It's the same gravity that operates on a prior assumption and makes coherence out of what is incoherent. I have begun to love myself. I've learned to give myself the permissions and affirmation I never knew as a child. God. Word made flesh, already and not yet. The reminders were in the woodpile after hours of stacking. They came in the hay when the sheep were hungry. They were in the wind and sand. They spoke of God, reconciler and healer. That special secret you couldn't wait to tell your friend in the dark after the abbey lights went out, the wind howled louder, and waves crashed like thunder on the sand.

3

Zombies

I'M EVOLVING. I DON'T do things to make them ego satisfying. Being a person of faith probably has something to do with it. But it's really about grace.

Grace is where beauty begins. It means having an identity—not perfect but growing and changing and evolving. Have we just met? Let's get to know each other. Let's not have a charcuterie party where everyone sits around and snacks on phoniness. I'm evolving in an interesting way, able to shine light into dark places. It's because of grace. It takes courage to recognize it, to make friends with it. It doesn't come from you and that is profoundly unsettling for people who live for their own ego. Grace comes from something bigger than you. It's meaningful when life sucks. It means you've made mistakes. It means you take responsibility for your actions instead of beating your chest to show others you are the dominant primate. Grace says yes to your mistakes. It hugs your trauma. Grace has an Architect. Am I right?

Grace threatens people who scapegoat others, narcissists without a self. They reject the human condition, that everyone is terribly susceptible to injury, themselves included.

I read something about this by Dietrich Bonhoeffer. He was a Lutheran pastor, imprisoned by Nazis as an enemy of the state. In the concentration camp he began writing about the moral and spiritual decay that made Nazism possible. How on earth did it happen? Nazism happened because of *stupidity*, or more accurately, stupid people. This has nothing to do with intelligence. Stupid people might be brilliant or sophisticated. What makes them different is how they refuse personal responsibility. They have no self. They won't reflect, won't consider the consequences of their actions in terms of others. Without a self they are morally and spiritually bankrupt. They are immune to guilt–you know, that feeling which helps little kids learn basic courtesy and respect. The stupid person does not put himself in others' shoes. He can't understand why anyone would want to. The stupid person is a liar. He becomes conditioned by lies to the point of reshaping beliefs, losing the ability to distinguish truth from fiction. Here is the kicker. The stupid person, living without grace or God or anything bigger than himself, befriends evil. The stupid person might not be directly involved in the effort to scapegoat and kill every remaining Jewish person, but she is untroubled by it. She applauds it. The stupid person is *available* to evil. She is terrified that others will discover how empty she really is. You see, it's easier to blame or scapegoat others than confront your own emptiness. I wonder if Bonhoeffer knew about zombies. Stupid people are zombies, looking to eat anyone with a self or grace. I think we've already experienced the zombie apocalypse. It looked like Nazi Germany.

You've got to have a self to see grace, to recognize it. I was in Australia working with the disabled. One evening I walked across a famous bridge. It was one hundred percent epic. This bridge is near the opera house in Sydney harbor. It is massive and huge and imposing. I was there with two other people including Lawrence, a disabled gentleman. Without warning, the fireworks started. It wasn't a holiday, at least to my knowledge. But it was incredible. It was the most unexpected, spontaneous, *beautiful* moment. I was surprised by grace. Bowled over. My friend Lawrence was experiencing awe. He was overwhelmed by the magnificence of that display. He was showing me something, the importance of wonder and awe. God was present. I was swept up into the richness of sharing this incredible event with other people. It was like everything good in the world was happening at that single moment, a point at the center of a radial web of converging circumstances which together became grace. I'm not a very good storyteller. I'm not explaining well. Maybe I should talk about it in terms of feelings?

After college I got to see Mother Teresa. She was getting an honorary degree at a nearby university. This school had an institute which made a big deal out of peacemaking and service with the poor. My neighbor friend asked me if I was going to see Mother Teresa. We were living across the street from the university. It took some badgering before I agreed to go. We didn't have tickets, so we had to fake it. We joined a procession outside the conference center. The building was crammed with people. The overflow numbered in the many hundreds, spilling out into the street. So, I'm standing there with four hundred people on the sidewalk, and she comes walking along, wearing her white robes with blue stripes. She's a tiny thing. She's this little nut-brown woman with eyes I had never seen before. They were eyes of kindness, of grace. She turned and looked directly at me. It was like someone told her at that precise moment to look absolutely and firmly into my eyes. It went right through to my soul. I could not believe it. There wasn't a single word that passed between us. I was opened to grace. In the lecture she talked about how you don't have to travel to Africa or India to make a difference. The poor and oppressed are right in front of you. Right *here*. Who in your neighborhood is hungry? Who needs to move into recovery? Go there first. You don't have to come to India. Do what is loving, do what is compassionate right now. Stop stressing about it. Sometimes we make it too complicated. Am I right?

At the time I was caring for my aunt. My mother had recently died. It felt like my inheritance was not about money but about a role, that of a caregiver. Mother Teresa was speaking into the remote corners of my life. She was validating what I was trying to do. Validation wasn't coming from other places, at least during that time. I wasn't getting it from mentors or family members. She was a conduit for something much larger than us. God the Father. Jesus the Son. The Holy Spirit. I read an interview with her afterward. Her comments were simple and direct. "I don't see crowds. I see individuals." I wanted to dance. I wanted to shout and say I know you do! You saw me. I didn't wear anything special. I didn't do anything special. I hadn't showered or brushed my hair. There was leftover broccoli in my teeth. On a whim I stumbled out of the kitchen and went to the university. You saw me, you loved me. It was grace.

4

One Eye

Who is God? It's a great question. Faith was a big deal for my parents. Kneeling beside the bed, I can still see them. Mass and confession and not eating meat on Fridays and all those kinds of things. They weren't stupid about it. They had a good solid sense of it. Do you know the Baltimore Catechism? It was one of those check-the-box catechisms. It was very rote, from well before the 1950s. I remember my teacher had us going through this material. At a certain age I thought, *I don't think this is what faith is*. So, I refused to do it. I refused to memorize the catechism because that was not what faith was about. I got sent home. I was punished by the principal.

I told my parents why I was sent home. I didn't know what to expect but I remember my mom and dad were like, you are right. We don't think faith should be evaluated based on your ability to repeat back these memorized things. That isn't who God is. That isn't what faith is about. I'll never forget sitting at the dinner table and telling them what happened, and they told me I had taught them something. Amazing. I couldn't believe it.

They were like that. It saddened them when they saw their kids grow up and weren't interested in going to church. It took everybody time. My parents were patient with us, but they would pull out their hair. On Good Friday you were supposed to sit at home and look glum and instead we'd go see a movie. My mom was hilarious. She'd hunch over and shake her head. My God, I can't believe it. A *movie*.

I've been a priest for a long time. Back in the beginning, especially when I started this gang outreach thing, I would be riding my bike in the middle of the night and come across something and say, "Hey, put down that Uzi." There was a lot of craziness, people threatening to kill each other, right out in the open. A lot of it was totally immediate. A lot of it was super stressful. But I was wide-eyed and idealistic. God respects you. God values you. How else would they hear and understand? You think back on those days when somebody would come to you and want to talk about whatever problem they were going through. You would spend a couple of hours with them. I miss that.

When I am here, there is a list of people to see. You have to triage and move as quickly as you can. Not that you get cynical as time goes on, although you're a little more clear and you can detect things. Your bullshit detector is high and that has been true for me. It's hard to pull one over on me. We had a groundbreaking yesterday for our new headquarters. It's been a big deal to move the whole enterprise to a new location, which I hope will be our last location. It will change the face of this place. I've had a lot of health issues. I was diagnosed with leukemia and I went through chemo and this will surely come back. I'd like to tie up loose ends before I go anywhere.

The tricky thing about this place is that the engagement level is high. In the course of a day, you can have your heart broken, you can be enormously frustrated and you can be in the vicinity of high hilarity, sometimes in the same half-hour period. It's one of those things I wouldn't trade, ever. To be engaged at that level is never boring. It's never dull.

I hope we will have a solid footing in the community, that it becomes a place where African American and Mexican gang members from all over LA County can get help and redirect their lives and move on. I hope that will happen. I want to be a calm, steady presence here. Kind. I want to go where love hasn't arrived yet. That's who God is. That's what God does. I want to stand with the people on the margins whose dignity has been denied. Stand with people who have been left out and demonized, the least likely to succeed. I don't want to change who I stand with just to have a better shot at success. I want to make it simple, anchored in kindness. One person at a time, one day at a time. No big, grand schemes. Less complicated.

God is an old shoe. Comfortable. He can't take his eyes off me. I appreciate that. It's never feeling like I've let God down. It's not that. In the last fifteen years, it's been a deep sense that it's God's joy to love me. I don't think I ever thought about that before. Maybe God loves me, but it's sort of begrudging and half-hearted. When push comes to shove, he probably does love me. That came late in my life. I'd been a Jesuit for a long time. Then, out of the blue, it clicked. I thought, *it's his joy to love me. Behold the one beholding you and smiling.* That's different from the one-bad-step kind of God who has you looking over your shoulder. I don't have any sense of that anymore. It's like the warm sun on your face, sitting in the cool summer breeze and letting it fall right over you, bathe right over you. That's what it's like for me.

God is compassion. God is loving-kindness. I think we're asked to be in the world, so it's a question of refining who God is in your mind. Ignatius used to say that God is always greater, so when you start to land on something you recognize, you see how it lines up with who God is. You like it and it feels good. It helps you visualize and conceptualize.

Here is an image I have of God. A dear friend of mine, his father was dying of cancer. He stopped his ministry as a Jesuit to take care of his father. It was total care. It was bathing, carrying him from his bed, feeding him, dressing him. At night he would read him to sleep in much the same way that his father used to read to him when he was a kid. It was a role reversal that happens when you take care of your parents when they're dying. He put his father to bed, a man who had shriveled away to eighty-five pounds with cancer but was still attentive and alert. Mentally, he was all there. The father would lie in bed and smile at his kid, you know. This friend would try reading him to sleep and the father would stare at him and smile. When my friend would look up from the book, he would say, "Come on! Fall asleep. Work with me! The idea is you're supposed to fall asleep. I read and you fall asleep. Get it?" His father was this impish, Irish guy. He tried to close his eyes, but he couldn't keep them closed. They would pop open again, even just one eye. He would be staring at his kid. My friend would go through this again and again–you're *killing* me. I'm exhausted. This went on and on.

After his father died, my friend looked back and realized what was going on. His father loved him so completely he couldn't take his eye off him.

That's who God is for me. You have to nurture it and foster it and keep it in view. Behold the One beholding you and smiling. The voice breaking through the clouds saying, "You're my beloved in whom I am wonderfully pleased." That's the only thing God wants to say to us. It's never about reminding us how much we screwed up, how badly we came up short. God will not be enfeebled by what enfeebles us.

5

Intention

THE MEANING OF LIFE is intention. I learned about this from a woman in my church. She was homebound for twelve years with horrific pain. Of all things, she was a nurse. She had a terrible back surgery, botched and worse. Despite all this, she was a prayer champion. She was in pain twenty-four hours a day and she often wondered why God did not take her home. But she had intention. Or maybe it's better to say she had intentionality. She lived intentionally. She was a person with eternal, prayerful intentions. She kept going, she kept praying. I do not want to exist without an intention, or a sense of intentionality. Even if I should end up a vegetable or in a situation like hers, I would hope that I could be a prayer champion, to have the same intention.

I'm learning, sometimes very slowly. Three years ago, I nearly walked away. I had a lot of regret. I had burnout. I regretted ever going into non-profit administration. I was sorry I spent all those years in grad school. The debt, the time, the sacrifice. It took a while to move through the regret, to find an intention once more. It took a while to ask for what I wanted and needed, or what was important. I prayed and prayed and prayed to become a social worker. Finally, I have been doing it. But it's happening on God's terms. I don't work in a cushy suburban office. I split my time between a level 1 trauma center and a non-profit that provides emergency services to the poor. Social work is challenging and hectic. Without intention, this work will destroy you.

I learn about intention from my cases. They inspire you, like that nurse with the scrambled back. There was a young boy who came into the ER one evening. His left hand was mangled. It was heartbreaking. He had found the key to his father's safe, opened it, and found a loaded handgun. He was preparing to shoot himself but instead shot off much of his left hand. This eight-year-old boy came into the trauma center with big eyes, in shock. Shock is weird. Sometimes it works to your advantage, shutting off pain and protecting higher mental function. The doctors were sweating and working to save what they could of his hand. Partly to distract him, I pulled up a stool, got to his level and started talking.

In a calm voice he told me his family came to the United States from Sinaloa in Mexico, to get away from cartel violence. His parents had worked very hard to get papers, to bring him across the border. They rented a house in Calipatria and managed to get him a trampoline. Then his parents told him they were divorcing. His mother would move to Arizona to be close to her sister. He would remain with his father until the divorce was final. This little boy was convinced the divorce was his fault.

He and I worked together for a long time. He kept saying I was the only person who could help him. It's trauma bonding. Children are concrete. They don't think in abstractions. It's hard for them to understand something abstract and complicated like divorce. It's easier for the child to blame himself. This was the starting point for our work together. He began to realize he had value. He was unsure of his parents' love, but he became very sure of mine. He began thinking about why God had spared his life. It became his intention.

Why *did* God spare him? Maybe God knew his dog would be sad if he were gone. Maybe God spared him to make sure his teacher knew the truth about another boy who had been cheating. Maybe God protected him because he was a good hitter and his baseball team needed him. Maybe God kept him safe to make sure the trash went out. This went on for several months. Then he announced that he had figured out why God had spared him.

"God spared me because he gets happy when I take communion."

It was this young boy's intention to worship God. I have never seen anything like it. His intention was completely pure. Even though this was a conversation about God, his intention was concrete. This might be some kind of cosmological secret. We don't need to be spiritual rock stars or theologians or whatever. The simple act of receiving the blessed sacrament. As an intention, it changes everything.

This boy taught me so many things about myself. He flipped the script. He showed me things are better when they are concrete. For as long as I can remember I've wanted to give my all to God. I had ridiculously convoluted arguments for why. Have you ever guilted yourself into a decision or action? That's not from God. All I am doing is shaping myself to the expectations of others.

Intentions are best if they are left concrete. Stop going on about abstractions like burnout. Stop making everything a dissertation. God spared me because he gets happy when I take communion.

I am a late bloomer—but I am blooming. I'm always learning and ready to repent and make changes. I'm awfully slow and plenty thick. But I have intention. A lot of people my age would not be trying to start a new career, especially social work. I try to practice forgiveness. This matters in our relations with others. The harder aspect is me. I am learning to stop and recognize pain. I am learning to forgive myself.

Intentionality is so much harder because of my struggles to forgive myself. I'm a perfectionist. I won the top award for my class of four thousand undergraduates at UC Irvine, the best student in any major. I hold myself to crazy standards, way too high. It's my biggest struggle. It puts me in the driver's seat, pushes God out of that seat. I've had some success with Ignatian practices—prayer, listening, and discernment. Learning to see how I'm part of the problem while at the same time trying to see myself the way God looks at me. I have a lot to forgive myself for. That bondage you are experiencing comes from not forgiving. When we forgive someone else, changes take place in that person even if you do not meet with them or they are thousands of miles away. The same is true when we forgive ourselves. It's intentional change. Accepting myself in my weakness. In my weakness, I am made strong in Christ.

When I meet with people in a social work setting, forgiveness is always the issue. God is a God of forgiveness. Let go and forgive. You do not have to continue in that relationship with an abusive person. I can talk with them and help them with forgiveness. A few cannot. They just can't do it. They get stuck. But for others it does happen, even if it's a long, slow process. The hardest is self-forgiveness. It's tragic. Abused women or children who cannot forgive themselves. I try to help them while I am struggling with it too. Perhaps this is why we have relationships that require forgiveness. We can learn by doing, by creating habits. We can translate forgiveness in the external world into something that is internal.

When it becomes internal, it can become an intention. This is why God gets happy when I make a habit of communion.

My earliest memory came through prayer. I wrote about it in a magazine article a few years ago. I think this is why intention is so important to me. My family is from Taiwan. Most Americans don't understand what that means. People from Taiwan are the Chinese holdouts, the ones who wouldn't accept communism. For decades there's been fear of China invading Taiwan and getting even. My parents emigrated to California when I was four years old. I don't remember much, but I'm sure it was stressful. My prayer memory is about Jesus. He came through the front door at church. He looked right at me and smiled and came over and picked me up and threw me into the air like a papa. He put me on his shoulders and walked me to a pew where I could kneel with my parents. His intention was clear, "I'm here for you, right now and always. This is my house. Come and spend time with me."

I am very Trinitarian. I pray in the name of the Father and Son and Holy Spirit. I go to a bible study on Monday night. We study the bible verse by verse, trying to let scripture interpret scripture. It's giving me a bigger sense of understanding God. It's become an intention, to read the bible from cover to cover. Bringing it all together with the teachings of the Church.

When I look at Jesus, I see the balance he had in his life. He would go away and pray and be alone with the Father and then he would go and teach people. He would intentionally pray and then he would go and heal people. He would intentionally be alone and then he would minister to people. He modeled that for us. To be mature Christians we need to have that balance. We need to be alone with the Father. We need to find that rhythm of intentionality. If I go away and live as a nun and never come out, I still need this balance. I cannot keep going like the Energizer bunny three hundred and sixty-five days a year.

While she was alive Mother Teresa was the most admired person in the world. People would go and work with her and be changed. They would see how she had intentionally turned her life over to God. How many of us could do that? I could not live in Calcutta and take dying people full of maggots off the street. I'm a compassionate person. But I do not think I could do that. Mother Teresa had intention. She was mature in the ministry she was called to. It was her intention to participate in what God was already doing. Her every act became a response to God in real time. When we live this way, we are living out what happens when we take communion. It keeps things real, keeps them concrete. It makes God happy.

6

Hit Person

I AM A HIT person.

I get hit all the time. When I get hit, it's tough stuff. I get hit with a call to trauma room. I am a nurse practitioner. The hit is always about injuries. I have to deal with pain and grieving. Not just the patient, but my own. Be careful. Education opens you to crazy service. Kingdom service. Difficult service. When you say yes to God, you are saying yes to things with eternal implication. The stakes are big. Bigger than you. Much bigger than me. I carry forward even though I have plenty to do without being a hit person. My growth is realizing I did not go to school to do that. If I want to give my best, I need to listen to what God is calling me to do, not what everybody else is telling me to do. I am trying to get out of being a hit person. I want to teach kids in classrooms. I like to teach. But my life is not about me.

Ten years ago, I was locked into being a hit person. I kept trying to get out. I try to focus on things I want to do. Then I get hit over and over with patients. Those were not my best years. I was suffering from overwork. It was rough at church. We had a dysfunctional pastor. He was a very traditional Korean man. He did not think women should be professional. It's like your family from when you were little. Growing up in an extremely dysfunctional family. I was responsible at twelve years old for my stepbrother. No one would take care of him. So, I became responsible and overly responsible. Now it makes it hard to say no to the hit.

It's old stuff. I can tell a story. My faith and confidence in God goes far back. The Holy Spirit took me back to a year and a half old. The Spirit revealed to me God's hand and love in my early years. Extreme emotion. One of the most is gratitude. Thanksgiving to God. As a seven-year-old I started going to church on my own. That is where I needed to be. I needed to be in God's house. I had a sense of worship and being loved by the people of God. I was seven and at church on my own. How many churches today would wrap their arms around a seven-year-old Korean girl that walks in from the street? Where is your mother? They never ask me that. They just received me.

Deep gratitude for God to lift me out of a pit. To experience healing from wounds that go back all the way. You experience emotion at a high level. You feel them at a deep level. I am not manic depressant. None of those things. I experienced highs and lows. This is all part of faith. What did not change was this—a deep sense of being loved. I had a sense of the church and worship and being loved and this sense of home. My real home was not a safe place.

My mother was a paranoid schizophrenic. We did not know until I married my husband. The doctors say, "You got to get her to the mental hospital." We do not understand what was wrong with her. She left my father when I was four. My father stayed in Korea. I only saw him three times. He committed suicide. Shot himself in the head with a gun. My mother remarried in this country. She married an alcoholic. You can't bond with a paranoid schizophrenic. There is nothing to connect with. Growing up we thought she did not love us.

We knew she did not.

It stays with you. I remember moving to Koreatown. I had a baby and a toddler. My younger brother came to live with us. He was sixteen years old. We were all living together with my husband. A very tiny house. We lived together while we were remodeling it. My husband had gotten a new business. We moved to be closer to his work. There were seven crises going on. My mother had been trying to elude us. She knew we were getting her committed. My younger brother came to live with us right at this moment.

I am trying to raise little kids. I do it on my own because my husband has a new business. The house is a mess. I was alone a certain amount every day. I was going to my knees in prayer every day. Weeping. God, you have to help me because I do not know how to do this. I do not know how to be a mother for a sixteen-year-old who is not used to any discipline. This went on for months, deep weeping.

Then one day I remember the Matthew scripture. I memorized it as a child. *Ask and you will receive, seek and you will find, knock and the door will be opened to you.* So, this got me to join my church. I'm sitting about third row back on the right-hand side. The pastor was named Andrew. His sermon was about second-hand saints. They are the broken ones. God's strength works in them only because of weakness. I bowed my head and prayed a prayer of repentance. *God I am nothing but a second-hand saint. This prayer will tell you how overly responsible I was.* The tears began to flow but nobody saw the tears. At that moment I remembered people in the church when I was seven. These people parented me. They cared for me and showed me love. I had forgotten them. I had forgotten how much God loves me, that he has a purpose for me. So, it was deciding to follow Christ. Accept this love once more and prepare. I ended up going to college. Ended up in nursing graduate school to become a practitioner. It was a deep sense of peace even though I was still a very dysfunctional person. A very wounded person.

I think my mother was jealous of me. She suffocated the firstborn, my brother. He was the firstborn grandson. Very important in Korean culture. He drowned accidentally at two. Some of her behavior probably came from her childhood. They guarded her closely as a child. It did not help her. She was a high-risk kind of person. Her parents would not allow her to swim, so she would sneak off and swim. The way they hovered was helping her toward this illness. I do not totally understand the schizophrenia. I think there is a bent toward it. Maybe there is a gene. But also a behavioral pattern in the family.

She told me she never wanted children. Perhaps she should not have children. With my younger brother, she rejected him. I did not really exist. I did not exist until there was a reason for me to exist. The reason was to help her life be easier. I did not exist other than what she needed. My stepfather tried to love me. He loved with the best ability he could, under the circumstances. He had hardly any education. You can see why God would give me the gift of faith very young because I would not have survived without it.

God lifted me out of this dysfunctional family so that I would become a follower. This impacted others, including my younger brother. It impacted my kids and my husband. I still do not know the whole big picture. But it began to work through forgiving my mom. It was God's hand. It's complicated. I will not tell you all of it because we will be here forever. God helped me to forgive my mom and give me people who were discerning that could keep me on target as I went through it.

Do you see? Pain pushes us towards God. If I did not have hor-rific pain I would not have been pushed towards faith. Have you ever met people who are superficial? They never had trauma. They grew up and had everything. They are not very deep and they are self-focused. Embittered. Toxic person with entitlement. God gave me a gift of faith. I do not know whether he gave it to me in the womb. Or at seven years old. But it says that I am of great value to God.

My younger brother and I talk a lot about pain. When grow-ing up, we did not have anybody telling us how to live. How to make decisions. There was not anybody there to give us the teach-ing. What I got in the church. My brother and I talk about how we desire truth. When we find the truth, we think you want to know the truth.

Here is the truth.

The truth is *relationship*. It's not only about true or false. Christ says I am the truth. This truth is freedom not from pain but relating to the truth. Relationship with truth to live our best life. God is wow. I am living in eternity now.

7

Casino

I'VE HAD ISSUES WITH Mary. I don't mean that too seriously. Then again, maybe I do. I did stand-up comedy in college, so watch out. Comedians are like onions. We have layers. We smell. We might make you cry. If you can get past that, we are fantastic in whatever you are making for dinner.

Don't get me wrong. I value Mary tremendously. She has a very important place in the Church. When I took vows as a religious sister, I thought of her as a mentor. I wanted to be like her. Then I went through a period where I kind of ignored her. I was in Africa working with the former child soldiers of Joseph Kony, an unimaginable butcher. These were kids who had been enslaved, forced to kill. I struggled to understand where God had gone during their abductions. I've slowly come around to Mary once again. I'm regaining my footing after that experience. Pray for these kids who are now adults. There aren't words to describe what they have been through.

Recently I was helping with the funeral of a priest. He was a beloved guy, a dear friend and gift to the community. I had ordered flowers for the altar, a bunch of white roses. This well-dressed man comes right up to me after the funeral. I'd never seen him before. He wore an Italian suit and looked like a distinguished professor or George Clooney. With the greatest respect he asks me if he could take one of the roses. I said, "That's fine. Take whatever you want."

He points to the statue of Mary next to the baptismal font. "I'm a Muslim but I love Mary. I come in here and talk to her sometimes."

Wow. I was not expecting that. A thought went through my head like a lightning bolt. *I wonder if Mary is a door to God's humanity in Christ? Maybe she is opening spiritual doors for people in unexpected ways.* I had been keeping her tucked away in the closet of my spirituality. But this Muslim man got me thinking. Mary is the preeminent person in the communion of saints. She's not a female god. She is the mother of God. She is our spiritual mother. I realized it was time for Mary. I needed a structured way of reclaiming her.

That Muslim man's words really got to me. There's something about these archetypes that appeal to a deep, primordial place we can't reach. Praying the rosary has become a daily practice again. God talks to me when I'm praying it. I have a strong visual of the whole thing. The rosary is a hand-held journey, like a watercolor where beautiful shades of blue and red and green and yellow overlap and blend into each other to mark our spiritual steps. Maybe God laid it out like this because we need beauty after seeing so much horror and filth. It's like taking a hike in the old growth forest. Very quiet, achingly beautiful. It smells glorious. One step literally melts into the next. If you move backward to get some perspective, you will see a glow to the entire thing. There is a gentle pull toward each step. The next rosary bead is waiting to surprise you.

How do I cope with what I saw in Africa? Thank you for asking. I'm still figuring it out. Each day I work through it while I walk the steps. God is completely beyond my understanding. God's time is not my time. God is caring, God is palpable. God is not—me. God has a sense of humor. Thank God! God is available to every miserable moment on this planet. I don't believe God causes miserable things to happen. That makes me crazy, especially when people lower the bar and say, "God must have wanted X to happen." Or, "God allowed X to happen." I think about it more in terms of prayer. Everyone wants to pray laundry list prayers. I'm careful to avoid the laundromat. I try instead to hold each person in love, in my mind, and then let things evaporate back to God.

I look for what God is doing in the moment and make a personal decision to enter into it. God knew about that person or situation from before the beginning of time. Who am I to take control? Let go. Participate.

Much as I don't personally like it, I believe that people need structure. The Church provides this structure. It keeps me grounded, gives me something to hold onto. Did you ever see those old newsreel clips from Las Vegas in the 1960s, where there's a big casino and they're going to implode it? You probably remember the news clip with the Brylcreem narrator, that slick guy with a deep voice who is always talking about progress. They blew up the first Vegas Mirage casino. They used explosives and made it implode upon itself. There was lots of boom and lots of dust and lots of rubble and lots of sky-blue paint. Probably lots of asbestos! They were deconstructing the casino because it was time to build a new one. Sometimes the Church goes through implosions like this. God is faithful to rebuild and make it whole. God makes us new. The Holy Spirit restructures things because we need a good scaffold for the Kingdom.

I take comfort that we are a global Church. God hasn't given up on us, even if we are imploding in some parts of the world. The Catholic Church is universal. Sometimes it's hard to see from our American perspective. The Pope might come from Caracas, the Pope might come from Manila, the Pope might come from Lagos. God will rebuild us, even if there are things that must go. It's Mary's time. It's the right time to reclaim those parts of our tradition that we've neglected or haven't bothered to understand. We are Christ's Church. Didn't Jesus say we have to be pruned to become more fruitful?

8

Recovery

I GUESS RECOVERY STARTED in high school, even though I wasn't addicted to anything yet. My football coach called me a lazy stealing Mexican. Everyone on the team heard it. This is where the obsessive drive began, to show the coach and my team that I was better than lazy or stealing. It was a compulsion to do things and achieve things and it started right on the field. By nature, I am a competitive person. Sometimes I can be sensitive to perceived slights. But that coach made me aware of appearances. He was watching me. He was holding me to a different standard. When you are a kid, you don't understand that his standard was an impossible standard. In his mind you are always going to be a lazy illegal, even though my family is one hundred percent legal. I have endurance and drive. That racist coach and my own achiever mentality were a wicked combination. I obsessively worked and practiced and could not get him to play me in a single game. The obsession began to define my life as an identity. But even then, I knew there was more. Over time I discovered that naming the obsession takes away its power. So, recovery is about naming the hurt or whatever it is that keeps us from growing into God's ideal for us.

I am a recovering alcoholic and have stayed good for sixteen years now. I'm enjoying this life, especially now that I am a grandfather. I have been married thirty-four years. But the old me is still inside. That obsessive and compulsive kid is still there. The anger will be there too, although I've since learned to name and befriend it. Part of recovery is learning you can't wish the anger away. Instead, you must attend to it right away, because it doesn't bring anything good in your life. I focus on the joy present in the moment.

I will say it's unusual, my life. I thank God for how things turned out. I came home one night at three in the morning. My wife was crying in bed. I couldn't figure out what the hell she was crying about. I wanted her to stop crying. She was making me mad. I was the one who was supposed to be miserable and hungover. But this was a tiny sign of how bad things had become. I was close to getting myself into a crime. For the first time I was consciously aware of the drinking. I began to understand the terrible price paid by my family, what they were getting or not getting from me. My oldest son was in middle school, old enough to throw a plate at my head. He let me have it with some bone china. That rang my bell for real, helped me realize the damage that happened because of my stuff, my compulsive and obsessive need to prove I was good enough. It was maybe the most important moment of my life. I literally went cold from that plate. It shattered into a million pieces. The damage was all over the kitchen floor, in the rug, under the fridge, even inside the dog bowl. A few days earlier the pastor had given a talk on Ezekiel, walking through the land of dry bones. For the first time I saw the shattered bones that I had created. I wasn't yet able to name feelings or attend to anything, but I could name the moment. It was an Ezekiel moment.

I understood in that moment how completely alone I was. Even though I had friends, I was totally isolated. What I was pursuing was worthless, meaningless. I was losing the respect of my family, the love of my wife. It was dry and hopeless and bitter. God spoke to me in a strange way during the Ezekiel moment. I am an accountant for work. At the time I worked for Deloitte, a big accounting firm here in LA. There was a colleague visiting from Toronto and it was early November. He came to our team meeting with this beautiful red poppy on his lapel. I asked him about it. He told me Canadians also had a Veterans' Day. They called it

Remembrance Day. Everyone wore the poppy as a sign of respect and remembrance. The idea came from a short poem written by a Canadian officer during one of the most horrendous battles of the First World War. It might have been the most awful battle in modern history–nearly one hundred thousand people died in the fields of western Belgium, gassed with chlorine and mutilated by shrapnel in the trenches. In the poem the dead are talking to the living in a field covered with the blood of soldiers from the British Commonwealth and France. Red poppies are growing over the dead, where there was no recourse or escape. I knew what God was saying to me. He was telling me I was a dead man walking. The battle was of my own making. The enemy was myself. The weapon was alcohol.

By the grace of God, I slowly stopped drinking. But I was still obsessed with things. For a time, I became a dry alcoholic. Then I started to recognize and name the obsessiveness. A new word crept into my thinking. G-R-O-W-T-H. Dead men can't grow anymore. Living men can. Poppies grow as a reminder of life that is still happening, made possible by the bravery of those dead Canadian soldiers. Growth became the motivation to go home and apologize to my wife and my sons. It moved me to apologize to my mom who was still an unrecovered alcoholic. The biggest growth happened in our backyard. I found my son digging in the dirt, hammering out his frustration and anger. I could see that he was digging a trench, like the battlefields in Belgium. How did he know? I sat next to him and asked what he was doing. No answer. Then I said it. "Son, I have nothing. I have failed you as a father. I am sorry. This whole thing is my fault."

For a long time, he didn't say anything. Then he looked at me. I will never forget the look. His eyes were full of pain and compassion at the same moment. "Yes. I still love you." Those words will be with me forever. Yes. I still love you. We sat together for a long time without speaking. He knew I was completely honest with him. He returned the favor and was honest with me. God redeemed my life from that battlefield trench. I grabbed a shovel and began digging with him. Together we decided the trench would become a goldfish pond. We dug for an entire week. Today the pond is a sacred place of recovery. There are California poppies which grow in golden bunches around the pond. It has become a place of remembrance.

My life was still a mess. I wanted to be a bachelor, wanted to be married, wanted to make lots of money, wanted to do whatever I wanted. All the time I didn't really know what I wanted. But growth had me and wouldn't let go. You know it wasn't growth by itself. It was God. I was surrendering to Christ's words. Yes. I still love you.

Much of the change happened because of the accident. My youngest son had mild epilepsy. Around this time, he was riding his bike home from the park and had a grand mal seizure. He'd never had a seizure like this before. He lost consciousness and crashed his bike, just as a city bus was going past. The bus driver had no chance, it happened too fast. The bus sideswiped the bike and my son's head was hit. I got the call that Jesse was at County USC with a fractured skull. I will never forget sitting in the waiting room with my wife and relatives, wondering if he would live. I was beside myself. I found the hospital chapel and got down on my knees. I prayed so hard my forehead was covered in sweat. *Please God, save my son.* I was bargaining with God, telling him to take my life, telling him that I would give money to the poor, telling him that I would go back to church and get my life right. After a long time, the doctors came out to the waiting room. A membrane around my son's brain had been torn, but he seemed to have all his faculties. They told me he would need to be closely monitored for a year, making sure there wasn't brain damage. The monitoring would help them know the extent of the epilepsy and his risk for another big seizure. I was electrified with hope and began going to church. For the next year I prayed like nobody's business. I got involved in a men's group, a fantastic place with guys that were hardworking, loved to play ball, and were committed to prayer. They were Christ to me. I was saved.

I got involved in an ethnic formation program at church. The biggest part of that program is about stripping away our defenses and discovering what's inside. Learning that it's good to name the obsessions before they do damage. I discovered it was possible for me to forgive others, even when people have treated me terribly. I began to go to A.A. meetings. One guy, a Chicano like me, stood up and told this hilarious story about an obsessive thing he did. While at the Home Depot, someone backed into his car and dented the bumper. He was pretty sure he knew who did it. He followed that dude all the way home to an apartment building. Then, my A.A. friend went back to his house. His wife was taking a shower. He literally yanked her out of the shower and took her, dripping wet with only a towel, down to the garage to show her the dent and tell her what happened. He was ready to take a sledgehammer and go to the other guy's apartment and put a dent in his truck. The wife took one look at the car. "Honey, there is no dent on your car." And she was right! We laughed for fifteen minutes straight because we all knew–that's *me*. It was a growth moment, a time to wear the poppy and remember. I went and told my wife the story and asked her forgiveness. There were many dents like this one in my life.

Do you know about the Jurupa Oak? Growth is humble, like that very old tree. It's not really a tree. It's a shrub that grows in the Inland Empire, on a hillside with chaparral that always seems to be on fire. The Jurupa Oak mostly lives underground and regrows from the same root after each wildfire. It's almost indestructible. The Jurupa Oak is one of the oldest living things on earth, more than thirteen thousand years old. The growth happens slowly and quietly. No one is clapping. There's no one watching, except God. We are placed on this earth by a loving God who designed us in his image. Our growth is not meant to bring glory to ourselves but to the God who made us. It's slow and quiet and beautiful. It is enduring and eternal.

When you are in A.A., you learn to accept that you are not God. This is a very big deal. Part of alcoholism and obsessiveness is atheism, pretending you can rise above appearances and create obsessive perfection that will make everyone else, like your coach or wife and kids, love and admire you. I heard a good one about this at A.A. The story goes there are two paradigm moments in human history. The first was when Galileo proved the earth was not the center of solar system. The second was when you looked at the mirror and realized you are not God. This is the deeper meaning of the Ezekiel moment. Back when I was pretending to be God, I was a terrible listener. I'd interrupt people and sometimes ignore them. Now, it seems like all I do is listen. I seek the advice of others. I read the scriptures. I listen to the Holy Spirit and wait until there is peace before I make an answer. If there is peace when I come to a decision, is the right decision.

Listen and watch and you will see what I mean. The grace of God glides through my brothers and sisters. It allows me to experience Christ. It allows me to experience humanity and to serve others. In the streets of LA are these wonderful classic buildings and people just outside sleeping in appliance boxes. They have terrible addictions and haven't yet been hit with the plate or found the poppies growing next to the pond. They haven't heard the words–Yes. I still love you. They haven't seen the Holy Spirit heal someone with epilepsy, make them whole so that never again will they have a grand mal seizure. When I'm ministering to the addicted it brings things home, it puts integrity over everything I've shared with you about recovery. In a small way I hope they will see the growth in me, someone who is one of their own, and choose life.

It's simple, really. It starts with another person's dignity. Showing they have worth. Christ was betrayed three times by Peter. What did he do in response? Three times Christ asks Peter whether he will care for the sheep, God's people who were forlorn and lost. Recovery is redemption that restores dignity, what it means to be made in God's image. Jesus redeems Peter, even though Peter publicly rejected the Lord and behaved like a professional atheist. Redemption can restore dignity. In one year, our nation spends enough money on defense to feed the planet. Can you imagine what would happen if we spent that money on hungry people? I would bet we'd no longer need missiles or aircraft carriers.

I focus on joy present in each moment. Not long ago I was reading to my grandson. I don't remember what was so funny, but he started laughing. At first it was a giggle. But then it grew into a belly laugh. I couldn't help myself. I started laughing too. We must have laughed for ten minutes straight. The laughter of a child is God's presence. Inside the laughter there's a quiet voice. Yes. I still love you.

9

Chitlins

DULAN'S IS THE BEST in town. They have spicy chitlins, just like gramma would make. It's off menu goodness. You have to ask for it. Chitlins are old time comfort food. My Haitian grandparents discovered it went perfect with red beans and dirty rice. Gramma would sometimes make it with collards and mustards. We'd have chitlins on Sundays often, right after Mass. I'm pretty fortunate to have grown up like that. When I was a kid, Louisiana was a Creole stew of different cultures and traditions.

Over Christmas break I was talking to my buddy on the phone. He's a lot like me—we like to cook and eat. Probably we like the eating part a little too much. We were talking about comfort food. Why is comfort food comforting? That was the question. It was an interesting conversation. I realized we need comfort food because life hurts. Life can sometimes go sideways. It can hurt bad. We might need a little comfort just to make it through the day. Comfort food warms everything when the cold wind is stabbing you. It makes you feel like you can face the suffering.

We discover comfort food as kids, about the time we learn that life hurts. I was raised by my mom because dad died when I was seven. While she was driving us to dad's funeral my mom's brother was killed in a car accident. So, there it was. In two days, my mom lost her husband and her brother. Later that week my grandfather—mom's dad—was diagnosed with cancer. One week after that my gramma, mom's mom, had a heart attack and passed. Over ten days, four huge tragedies came down on my poor mother. I was just a kid. But I had a glimmer that she was suffering. I will never forget seeing her cry.

From that point things changed. I sometimes had to be the parent because she got into some pretty serious drinking. She worked two jobs and did gigs on the side. She had a series of boyfriends. Some were abusive and I, unfortunately, had to get involved. That wasn't much fun. There were no questions about whether we were loved or whether we were the most important thing in her life. It's just that she had a tough time. Somewhere around then I remember discovering mac and cheese. I'd had it many times before. But I never made the connection—comfort food tastes best when life hurts the most.

Just last week I was in the storage unit going through pictures. I hadn't looked at those pictures in years. A lot of them were from the time my wife and I split up. I grabbed some baby pictures and made a folder for my youngest son because he was only two when we split. He doesn't remember his mom and me being together. Right now, he's going through some dark times. Not long ago one of his friends killed himself. So, I made this photo album with all these pictures of him as a kid, little baby pictures from the time he was born. Pictures he had never seen. He and I were sitting right here at Dulan's one month ago. We were able to laugh at the pictures. We laughed at how people dressed back in those days. We were laughing and we were eating. All this happened while we were eating smothered chicken. Somehow that chicken made the sun break through the darkness.

I've been a football coach at Crenshaw. I've been a youth minister. Now I'm a deacon. Back when I was doing youth ministry there was a kid whose dad was single, like me. I didn't know him well, but I knew the family. The dad hung himself. He left two sons and a daughter to be raised by relatives. It was devastating, to say the least. His funeral hit me hard because I understood his loneliness. I understood the depths of how despondent he could have been, knowing what it's like to have your family taken away by a lawyer. Knowing it's the same town but you don't get to tuck your kids in at night. It's something only a divorced guy can understand. The dad who killed himself was one of the nicest people I'd ever met. He was one of those people who never said a negative thing about anybody. He was good and generous. Nobody saw it coming.

His oldest son loved to cook. He was shy about it. He'd finished his junior year and his buddies were interested in football and girls, probably cars too. Nobody in his world was interested in cooking. This grieving kid knew that I liked to cook, and he trusted me. He'd found a used cookbook written by a gramma in North Carolina. He waited until the other kids were gone and then showed it to me. What a treasure. This little cookbook was full of incredible recipes. Everything was old time comfort food. There were recipes for pork chops and cornbread, liver and onions, country ribs, black eyed peas with hamhocks. Fried okra and bread pudding. Ham with redeye gravy. Meatloaf three ways. It went on and on. I asked this kid whether he'd tried any of the recipes. He shook his head. Then he looked up and said, "Do you think we could try making one together?"

He came over to my house the next Saturday. I asked him to pick a recipe. I told him we'd check it over, make a shopping list, and get to the store. It created a big problem because there were too many good recipes in the cookbook. We talked for almost an hour, pros and cons, this versus that. Apparently, he loved catfish and crawdads and all kinds of seafood. So, we decided on fried catfish and hushpuppies with turnip greens and butter pecan ice cream for dessert. We made an ingredient list and went shopping. I was worried we wouldn't be able to find some of the items, especially the greens. But it all came together. We took everything home and got cooking. We spent the whole afternoon cooking up a storm.

This poor kid was like a robot in the months after his dad's death. Going through the motions. Real suffering does that. When you are crushed, you are down and out and half-dead. All your creativity and dreams are drained right out of you. There was no light in this kid's eyes—until we began cooking that day. It was a little miracle. I'm not exaggerating. He became alive. He began singing and humming and telling stories. He was joking around, flicking food scraps at me and giving things to the dog. He shared a secret dream of opening his own seafood restaurant. I realized the comfort wasn't just in the final product. It was in the preparation that was required to make the food. Comfort food is much, much bigger than a meal. It's everything that makes it possible, some of which can take hours or days. You have to clean things and chop them. You might have to marinade overnight. Once the stove is hot and things are sizzling, you have to figure out whether it's ready and done. You have to do it without poisoning anyone or turning your expensive ingredients into a hockey puck. The process of making comfort food with that kid was a celebration. It was an act of reverence. It was the same feeling that comes over you when you realize you've been given a precious gift.

The whole thing became a feast. We prayed and gave thanks, and we ate. We high fived each other and ate more. We congratulated each other and ate until we were almost sick. The food turned out great, even fantastic. Dulan's was the target and we smacked it. Somehow that little cookbook from Carolina was able to touch this kid who was stuck in the darkest of places. Comfort food can do that. It can become a spiritual thing. It reminds us of home. I think these things are connected. When you're suffering it feels like you're lost. You don't feel like you have a home. A safe place where you can catch a break from the suffering. I'm not talking about home in terms of a building. I mean where we live spiritually, what it means to have a place that is totally blessed with God's love. I didn't know in the moment, but that kid had found a home in our relationship. There was comfort food at the center of it all.

That's not the end of it. God was making a new home for this kid's brother. His younger brother was in middle school. It took about a year for the change to happen. He went from being a good student and promising athlete to a kid who was dark and troubled. His struggles got worse all the way through high school. I got to know him during his sophomore year when he made varsity football. He was a good player, a first-string receiver who made a lot of catches for touchdowns. But his struggles haunted him on the field. He'd have anger meltdowns, sometimes cheap fouling the other players and costing us huge penalties. Once I had to bench him for a month when he started a fight after a game. You might say I had a relationship with this kid, but it was pretty different from his brother. More than once, I had to read him the riot act. I found out later he'd gotten into serious trouble with the law.

As a coach, I make a habit of going to graduation, even though I'm not involved in their lives as a teacher. After the ceremony, I look for the kids I coached or mentored. I ask whether they want to take a picture together. I took a picture with this kid right after his graduation. He said, "Coach, will you go to lunch with me at Dulan's tomorrow?" So, here we are at the restaurant. He is graduated and he's wearing new shades and he is smiling but I noticed there were drops falling on his shirt. He was crying. He was trying to tell me how much he appreciated what I had done for him. I didn't realize that I had done anything, really. I did for him what I would have done for any of my football kids. I'll never forget those tears falling on his shirt under his dark sunglasses while we were sitting here at Dulan's. You're probably wondering what we were eating. Short ribs, oxtails, and grits casserole. It was comfort food, the kind that reminds you of home.

He moved away to Atlanta a few years back, but we visit when he's in town. He ended up going to college and today works as an insurance agent. He makes good money and has a beautiful family. I'm so proud of him. I make a point of telling him that. Usually, it makes him tear up. He still has a home in our relationship.

I lost my best friend about a year ago to brain cancer. She got really sick. The whole thing happened over three months. I could talk about anything with her. She was always there for me–a total cheerleader. And it went both ways. She was the one who got me into youth ministry. She walked with me through the journey of becoming a deacon. She recognized something in me, something I didn't see in myself. I got to be with her family when she took her last breath in the hospital. I had never seen anyone die before. There was plenty of death in my world, but I never watched it happen. We didn't want her suffering and we were praying that she would go fast, and she did.

About a month after her diagnosis, I was helping our priest with the vigil Mass. It was a big deal for me, one of the first times I got invited to give the homily. You'd recognize the message, for sure. I told the story of that grieving kid who loved to cook, especially about how he found a spiritual home in our relationship. I talked about how the celebration and reverence that goes into the making of the food prepares us for relationship with God. The Eucharist, the body of Christ, is given as a reminder that God understands our suffering. In that sense, the wafer is a kind of comfort food, a precious gift that demands our attention and appreciation for the sacrifice of the cross.

Later I was administering the host for the assembly. Somehow my best friend ended up coming to me. When she bowed and reached out to receive the bread, it hit me like a brick. The Eucharist is more than a reminder that God appreciates and understands our suffering. Through the wafer Christ literally goes into the darkest parts of our being, those parts nobody wants to discuss or share, where things hurt the most. He finds the suffering down there and touches it, making it his own. This is incredibly personal and intimate. Through the Eucharist our suffering is being touched and redeemed by the God of the universe. Christ totally and completely identifies with our suffering. His body becomes part of ours, just like fried catfish and hushpuppies from that Carolina cookbook. It's not that hurt disappears in the moment. It's that the hurt is shared. You are no longer suffering alone. Christ is within you, united with it. I used to struggle to get my head around the word *solidarity*. Now I understand it. You are what you eat.

Giving my friend the Eucharist was like a revelation. It was like the scriptures about the burning bush or when the temple curtain was torn from the top down. When my friend took the bread, Christ was touching her cancer. He was putting his hands on what we all knew was coming, the terrible suffering when she'd pass away and our friendship would end.

Later that day I asked my friend what happened when she received the Eucharist. She told me it was incredible. She had a little vision when she took the bread. In her mind's eye, she and I were sharing a celebration dinner many years in the future. The restaurant was Dulan's. We were eating chitlins.

10

Authentic

WHEN I WAS IN junior high school, I met Donny Osmond. What a crush! My dad was friends with this promoter who managed to get the Osmond's to come to the San Fernando Valley. He told his buddy, "You've got this big Osmond fan here. Can you arrange it that she can go backstage?" And he did. We went back to the trailer and spent time with them. It was huge, but for reasons I did not expect. I discovered he wasn't really "Donny" backstage. He was Don—full stop. There was a serious difference between the TV product and the real guy. He was much shorter than he seemed on TV. He wore high-heeled platform shoes. Marie had so much makeup that I could barely see her eyes. She looked like a raccoon, almost. It wasn't what I anticipated. They were very subdued, like they had no energy compared to what you saw on TV. The entire thing shook me. I came to realize even smart and beautiful people can fall into a trap, living without fidelity to what makes you unique and precious.

Fast forward to my late twenties. I wasn't being authentic in the convent. I was trying to make myself into someone I wasn't. I was becoming a false self. I never, ever want to go back to that. I've read a lot of books on spirituality. I think there is such a thing as pseudo-spirituality, where you make spiritual claims that are borrowed from others. You use these to help sell an image of yourself to the public. I don't think it's real and I don't think it's healthy. I have an allergic reaction to that. It's kind of rigid, very plastic. It's a phony approach to sanctity and it's not real. I remember Jesus becoming upset with Pharisees and Sadducees over this.

I got a debilitating disease when I was in the convent. It was Lyme disease. I came close to death. It was disfiguring because I had something called Bell's palsy. My joints were completely messed up. Your energy absolutely bottoms out. I remember at the worst point, the act of sitting upright made me sweat bullets. People were trying to help by being funny. They were hilarious, but I was exhausted by the noise. Even though things were hideously awful, I was completely defenseless before God. I had no choice but let God love me. Looking back, I'm struck by how Lyme took away the extra measure of energy it takes to project a false self. When you are that sick, you must be authentically yourself, ready or not. That period of my life was a terrible time and a wonderful time at the very same time.

The Bell's palsy slowly went away and I started to get better. With Lyme disease, it's a recovery with fits and starts. The head nun was very hard on me. During meditation, we would sit around and reflect on the readings. At one point she started going on about posture and the importance of body posture when you pray. This was important and kneeling was unbelievably important. Somehow, not kneeling was insulting to God. I had stopped kneeling for a brief time because the doctor had told me not to put weight on my joints. This turned into serious blowback from the head nun. I felt so horrible I could hardly pray. I got so much flak that I called up the leader of the entire religious order and said, "I want to leave. I can't take this anymore."

Leaving wasn't easy. There was a lot of disorientation. I paid a price for authenticity. After the convent, I felt that I could breathe again. At the same time, I was couch surfing poor. I decided to stay in Long Beach and tough it out. I was hired by a priest who had been temporarily removed from national ministry. I know it sounds weird, but priests can get demoted just like any other professional. I found out he had gone through three directors of religious education in six months. I was number four. I applied for the job before I left the convent and immediately didn't like his behavior. He was misogynistic and abusive. He publicly humiliated me at a Mass. It was scary. I didn't have enough time on the job to acquire anything. I had zero financial stability. All I could do is trust God. So, I quit, and the Diocese offered me another position. It was a temporary thing, but it was enough for me to recover.

About this time, I had the opportunity to meet with the very last survivors from the Holocaust. We had Shabbat dinner with them. There was a man who sat next to me. He was sent to Auschwitz when he was thirteen. The commandant said to him, "How old are you?" There were two lines forming. The sick and young and old were in one line. He could see the good-looking, strong ones in another line. So, he lied about his age, saying he was seventeen to get out of the death line. The commandant didn't believe it, but my friend kept insisting, I can work! He got moved into the line for the living. At that point they weren't burning the bodies. They were digging pits and my friend's job was to drag the corpses and throw them in. Remember, he's thirteen years old. He's alone because his family was split up. On the spot he invented a prayer. *Dear God, I'm too young to have done pretty much good or bad with my life, but if you help me live, I will tell people about this place.* He didn't find meaning in what he was doing but he found a kind of meaning in his circumstances, which of course were awful. He discovered a purpose, to live authentically with what he was witnessing, to tell the truth about the horror. He discovered this purpose as life was ending for thousands of innocent people.

I will never forget that man. He was ancient and this was a few years back. He's not going to be with us much longer if he's with us at all. He made me promise to tell that story until I die. Hopefully, people will remember his authenticity. I can't forget his story and so I'm telling it now. He told me one other thing. He said every day he must purify himself. I took that to mean forgive, try to forgive. He told me that if you don't purify, you will become an animal. Even to that day, decades after Auschwitz, he knew the importance of forgiveness. Forgiveness kept the meaning of his story safe. Meaning can slip right out of our hands if we don't purify ourselves, or I think, forgive.

I believe God sees us exactly as we are. Authenticity is a defining characteristic of God. God loves us unconditionally, no matter how we are. God is always calling us to grow in love. We discover the hugeness of God's authentic love through other human beings. Being Catholic means connection with brothers and sisters who have gone before me in Christ. It's connection with brothers and sisters who are coming after me in Christ. I'm connected with brothers and sisters who are walking with me in Christ. I'm struck that God sees us as his beloved children. We are children bound by a divine love that is absolutely genuine and true. We are bound to each other and bound to the Trinity. This is probably the most gigantic, wonderful thing I can think of. What Catholicism means to me, most deeply, is that. The rituals are only meant to engage with what God is authentically sharing with us, how God is moving among us.

Authenticity is a kind of truth. It's mystical in that God affects it, but we have our own attitudes and our way of life. We can cooperate and respond, returning authenticity through our interactions with others. We can build on the gift of love that God has given and we can grow into it. Authenticity is a kind of solidarity with what's happening in the world right now. We have to be sensitive and honest with others. We have to do something. Maybe that's why God made us relational, more so than any other species.

I fell in love with this guy when I was in the convent. It blew fresh breath into my life, fresh air. Now, I didn't act out of that love, but it recharged my spirit. It was the first mature love that I had experienced, even though I had loved in a certain way before. I wanted to be with that person all the time. It was an incredibly strong experience of friendship. I talked to people about it. I went to see a woman for spiritual direction. I was dealing with my body clock going off, working those things out with her. I couldn't talk about it with my best friend. She would have thought that I left the convent because of him. Not true, it was more complicated. But this friendship opened my life in ways I didn't anticipate. I saw myself through his eyes and I saw how wonderful love really is, how exquisite it can be. He was authentic with me, which gave me new permission to be authentic with myself.

I'm learning to trust myself and let go of false spiritualities. I made the mistake of allowing the false spirituality run deep into my spirit. Now I am finding my way out. I've wondered if this is why Jesus gave us the Pope, an authentic reminder of God's love. I was lucky enough to see the Pope. My convent sisters and I were in the tenth row, in one of the stadiums. We saw him in New York. I don't know how to describe that experience, but it was remarkable. There was a huge attraction to it. It's an attraction to God. You could have heard a pin drop, even though it was a massive place and there were a lot of people. What he said gave us joy and enthusiasm. He was spontaneous, too. The wind was blowing super hard that day. It was sunny and windy and there he was talking about the Holy Spirit. Almost on cue, something blew over on the stage and he talked about the power of the Holy Spirit. Somehow, he made time change, made it sacred. It was transforming. It impressed me about how God loves us with complete sincerity and authenticity.

The Pope was tired and yet he was truthful with us, and he spoke with love. It wasn't this bland mamby pamby where anything goes, and I love you and you love me and everything is right with the world. He looked critically at us, our nation with its consumption and waste. Our enormous carbon footprint. His love stirred the love inside of us. This kind of love is authentically directive on a daily basis. The Pope said, "Don't be afraid. Don't be ashamed of Christ." He reminded us that Christ is real. Christ is coming again. It's what we already believe, but when someone really believes it, authentically believes it, there is a huge impact on everyone. Christianity is not a duty. It's belief—full stop. I've grown in that direction, maybe because of that experience.

I think that God cares about us like a mother would care about scribbly drawings that her daughter might do, or a father shows genuine interest in a model plane that was put together wrong by his son. There is a love and affection that is lavished upon our inadequacies. We only experience it when we are willing to receive that kind of mercy. I think that when we recognize it, we become open to the gift. It enlarges us. Then, we live out of the gift. Maybe there is a little bit more flavor in the world that wasn't there before.

Not very long ago I was walking on the beach with my sister and a guy named Alex. We were in my hometown of Ventura. Our feet were in the shallow water, at the trailing end of each wave. It was a beautiful night. The Pacific was warm and there was phosphorescence. It wasn't super dark but you could see the stars. You could see the water coming with each wave, glowing in the dark. It was a splendid moment, that wonderful feeling of being together. It was authentic. We were authentic. It was a joy to be there, to be washed over with authenticity.

Back in the convent, I thought that theology was the main way for me to grow. That was the proper path to spiritual maturity. You might think I'm nuts, but I now believe my growth depends more on cartoons. Yes! When you watch cartoons, you can see authentic human interactions. They are funny and slapstick. But you can learn from them. Of course, everything is staged, so it's more dramatic than what you'd see in real life. It has a beginning and an end, so it's easy to digest. I think cartoons can help develop an authentic understanding that is focused on a single area of growth. I'm working on my tendency to procrastinate. Road Runner and Wile E. Coyote are helping me grow beyond it.

When I was at Loyola, I was in a sorority and made some amazing friends. They challenged me on spiritual issues, especially the authenticity of love. They got me reading the saints. I love St. Thérèse of Lisieux. Are you familiar with her? She would practice her faith with these knotted beads where she would count the good things she had done throughout the day. I think this helped her keep on track, like a notebook of her offerings. She would say,

"I'm to God with empty hands." She would be seeking every opportunity, seeking to get the most out of everything which could be given back to God. She made everything a good gift. I think that's genuine faith. I am convinced of it. She gave joy and consolation to those who lost hope. When she was sick and going through that dark night, she would compose herself in such a way that was a preparation for heaven. She bore her own trial carefully so that it wouldn't drag anybody else down. Hers was a special kind of authenticity. It was a sign of mature faith. I think that kind of attentiveness and alertness is the fruit of mature faith.

Just last night I was driving back from Ventura. I started crying. I hardly ever cry. I was thanking God for the authenticity and goodness I find in my brothers and my sister. How they've grown into beautiful people. I'm still glowing from that drive. The Holy Spirit was passing over me with waves of authentic joy. I don't have words to describe what was happening. It was authentic reality— the beauty of God was on full display. It was explicit. Yes. That's the right word. It was an explicit evening. The mountains were explicit. The sunset was explicit. God's presence was explicit. It was about being together with my siblings. One of my favorite parts of St. Augustine's *Confessions* is when Augustine and his mom are together at the window in Lucia and they're looking out and talking about life and the future. Yesterday was like that. It was explicit.

11

The Turning Around

MY CONVERSION ENCOMPASSED MANY things. I was in my twenties, about twenty-five. I'd been married for six years. My life could be described as two kids and a troubled marriage. Out of the blue, my wife invited me to a charismatic church service. I had already blown off the Christianity thing. I had read the scriptures, New Age writings, Baghavad Gita, Koran, Buddhist texts. I knew more and I knew better. But the hidden truth was a tangled mess. I didn't have a clue about any of it. I didn't know myself or what I believed. And she had the audacity to invite me to this group of Jesus freaks!

It made me furious. No, I was enraged. I stormed off to the garage. I was refinishing a piano, which I must tell you, is a terrible project for someone who is angry. Pianos need love and tenderness. I was madly sanding and grinding it down, way too far, cutting deep into the heartwood. There was an earthquake while that was happening. Not a physical earthquake, but an internal break that split me wide open. Don't call me crazy, but I heard a child's voice in the moment. I don't know how to explain it. It was like a singsong nursery rhyme. The voice said, "Show this anger, show it and let it go." The shaking stopped. My rage vanished. In its place there was peace, and it was powerful. When you've been living for a long time in anger, you are slowly consumed. You forget what peace is, the elegant resolution of conflict. In the resolution we rediscover what is sacred and beautiful and eternally secure.

My life was changed as a result. It was a turning around. It was *the* turning around. What I turned to was the gospel. What I turned to was the person of Christ. What I turned to was the church and it welcomed me with hospitality and love and good boundaries. Strangely, I tried to shake it off over a period of two or three years. It sometimes felt like there was a hot thing sticking to me. It wasn't the heat of anger or rage. It was the radiating warmth of God's peace. I was a voluntary captive to peace. The turning around had nothing to do with me. It didn't happen because of my effort or strength of character. It was a surprise; the sort of encounter that is totally unexpected, like when you spin around and rediscover someone who has known you forever. God has been following you, one step behind.

I should give some context. I had a very rich, deep, and strong background in the Catholic faith as a kid growing up in England. Catholics are a disparaged minority in the Midlands. My mother was from the Central Belt of Scotland where Catholics are a tiny minority and persecuted even more severely. Looking back, I had a tremendous faith heritage. I haven't thought much about it until recently, but the rage went back to the conflict I sensed around me, the judgment and exclusion I felt as a kid because my family was Catholic. In the United Kingdom, Catholicism labels you. Everyone knows you have Celtic roots. Think Ireland. Potatoes. Famine. Second class citizens. Everyone knows how that story ends. For centuries there has been suspicion and hatred and conflict and blood all tangled in the troubles between Ireland and England.

I wouldn't have realized it as a child, but I understand now that I absorbed something about the faith that makes me Catholic without an accent, even though I became a Lutheran after the turning around. It got into semantic memory, a pre-cognitive catechesis. I got a Catholic sense of the sacred. I remember being six or seven and kneeling in the pew. I was kneeling beside my dad who always had a nice jacket on, always dressed up. He reeked of cheap cigarettes. I couldn't see much. But I was able to see this—the priest would hold his hands up and say, "Jesus is here" with absolute conviction. Now, I get it.

Jesus was right there in the garage by the piano. He was able to broker peace between the warring factions of my inner self, those parts that felt responsible for what I had done poorly and jealous for what I had abandoned. You see, I ran from England for America, leaving behind a good upbringing and opportunity to work with my father and take over his business.

The turning around brought the grace and peace of Christ into my life. But it wasn't easy. The divorce was terribly difficult. I don't have other divorces to which I could compare the one, but my former spouse was mentally ill from childhood. In hindsight, I can fully recognize it. At the time it was completely untenable. The divorce and the mechanics of it were enormously intense. I experienced a lot of distress in the process. I didn't want to have a failed marriage. I didn't want to let God down. I wanted to be there for my kids, even as they were stepping into adulthood.

Even after the divorce, it wasn't over. My ex-wife is bipolar. She has a delusional disorder and a somatoform disorder. Two of our four kids have the same diagnosis. Exactly the same. It was awful coming to terms with this truth. My youngest daughter, who is now twenty-five, had a psychotic break when she was quite young. It was terrifying and it was painful and it took months to accept she was mentally ill. No matter how much prayer, no matter how much hope, no matter how much whatever, it was like the apostle Paul. Please, *please* take this away from me.

This was happening while I was in my late thirties. A mentor at church was talking about reviewing our lives at the very end, asking questions about what we might look back upon with regret. What is God encouraging you to consider, but you will not? I wrote down, "Get an education." Shortly after I applied and miraculously got admitted to UCLA. At forty-one, I graduated. It was an incredible experience, walking in my cap and gown at forty-something. It changed my life. I don't mean the experience of graduating or achieving a goal. It was the epiphenomenal reality of getting an education. I didn't write "get a degree" or "get a career." I wrote, "get an education" in the literal sense of the word. The turning around made possible a new measure of self-respect which opened the door to education and subsequently changed my life. It gave me tools to work through my situation. To deal with it, recognize it, get the help needed. I majored in English and Psychology and Sociology. Three majors. God transformed me through the experience.

I married Sharon eight years ago. The week we were married she was diagnosed with stage four breast cancer. She wasn't expected to live. You would like to think that you can be altruistic, provide tender loving care and all of that. But you realize you just don't have it. You are weak and inadequate. All I had was love and the radiating warmth of God's peace, sticking to me like hot roofing tar. It made our communication more honest. We had great conversations that went far beyond what I thought possible for a relationship between two human beings. Before her last round of round of chemo we went up to the monastery. We looked back on where we'd been and what we had relinquished. She gently told me she was going to die and I would have to relinquish her. I will never forget that conversation.

In these moments of weakness, God dwells. God's indwelling changes me. It makes me realize that it is okay to ask for help. It says that I have limits. It says that I am fundamentally fragile and selfish. A man finds a treasure buried in a field. He buries it once more; relinquishes everything he has and buys the field.

12

Little Words

CHAPLAINCY IS LIKE MEDICAL practice. Spiritual care means avoiding harm, making sure my words don't make things worse. It can be tricky. We live in a strange time. It's a life after tradition. Many patients in my hospital have no religion or words to make sense about what is happening to them. Others are vulnerable. They have words but don't have strength to speak. With utmost care I sometimes use words on their behalf, mostly to protect them from people who are indifferent to what is really going on.

My friend Caleb was doing vanlife. He bought an old Dodge Sprinter and built a camper. He took the van through western North America, up to the Arctic Circle. For income he created a YouTube channel. He was doing seasonal work like picking beets and stuffing Amazon packages over the holidays. He spent a summer canning salmon in Alaska. He came back in October and went straight to the doctor. He'd lost sixty pounds. His complexion was grey, and he had no energy. The doctor told him it was liver cancer. He had three weeks left. Caleb ended up in my ward ten days later.

He was a Presbyterian, the son of a pastor. I knew him through our church. While Caleb was away, some acquaintances from that congregation had gone through a charismatic renewal. They heard he was sick and stormed the hospital during visiting hours. They were repeating strong words over and over, words like "fire" and "warfare." They brought guitars and were singing and laying hands on Caleb. In Jesus' name they demanded he get on his feet. It was egregious. These people weren't interested in Caleb. They were about themselves. They were stars in a show about divine miracles. They were posing for an unseen cameraman who might have been filming for Sundance.

Caleb couldn't speak. But his body was rigid with tension. His eyes were flashing. His thoughts and feelings were clear. Keeping a respectful tone, I asked the entourage to leave. They politely refused and I asked again. When they would not, I spoke before thinking. "Get. Out. Now. Quit your healing experiments and leave!" They were little words made bigger by the urgency of the moment.

That afternoon Caleb shared his thoughts on a notepad. The Holy Spirit had spoken to him after everyone left. God was going to heal him. But it wouldn't be here or now. It would be in person and face-to-face. Christ would lay his hands upon him as part of the journey from this world to the next. I asked how this made him feel. Caleb responded with a single word in pencil. "Reconciled."

He died the next day and his word changed me. I try to live each day within that word. I now believe reconciliation is God's ultimate goal for humanity, the endgame of existence. He created us. He loved us. It breaks God's heart when we're separated from him. There is nothing more precious to God than resolving this separation, restoring us to himself for eternity. The death and resurrection of Christ is reconciliation of all things human with a God of infinite concern.

My work is a ministry of reconciliation, even with those who are atheist or agnostic or uninterested. What's funny is the patients who see themselves as being outside the church expect me to defend the church. When it becomes clear I have no interest in defending anything, they suddenly have permission to become angry. Now we are getting somewhere. The first step toward reconciliation is honesty. If we can be honest about how we've been hurt and how we've hurt others, we may discover a reconciliation we never knew we needed. It's a reconciliation that matters more than anything else.

There are little words beneath reconciliation. They are the words of Jesus, words of love. Merciful. Forgiving. Enduring. These words help us understand ourselves. To the extent we understand ourselves, we become available for relationship. We get the memo—someone wants to know us. It might happen to be God.

One of my patients had breast cancer that metastasized to the bone. It was very painful. The doctors were giving her intravenous doses of pain medications. The meds weren't working. At some point it became obvious her pain was more spiritual than physical. She had a good marriage and wonderful kids but refused to talk about what was bothering her when they were in the room.

I gently asked her husband and family to give us space for some private talk. I did a guided imagery exercise with her. It's an exercise that puts the listener in the shoes of the blind man from Luke's gospel. The listener is supposed to hear Jesus' question, "What do you want me to do for you?" The listener becomes an imaginary surrogate for the gospel character, sharing the desperation of the situation and hearing Jesus' words of love and grace.

In the exercise my patient revealed she couldn't hear what Jesus was saying to her. She began to cry. She was afraid of dying because she wasn't good enough to get into heaven. This woman was a respected leader in her church, a person with a beautifully formed and vibrant faith. I shared with her scripture texts of assurance, including that incredible moment between Jesus and the Samaritan woman in John's gospel. It made no difference. There was a barrier to reconciliation in this woman's life. What could it be?

I took a great risk. I asked her if she'd been abused as a child. There was a long pause. Her answer was yes. She'd held the secret for more than fifty years. She told me the entire story. Somehow her words were able to break things free, making reconciliation possible. I only listened and pointed to her words. She began to accept that she'd done nothing wrong. While this was happening her pain level was going down. Eventually she no longer needed the meds. She began to hear Jesus speaking to her through the guided imagery. His words were reconciling words of affirmation and promise. She died in peace three days later.

What do You Want Me to Do for You

I'm not asked by God to provide wisdom. I'm called to listen. I wait for little words, for that quiet voice which speaks from eternity. This is guidance. This is discernment. Only with little words can I ask difficult questions that nobody else is willing to ask. They must be asked with utmost compassion and respect, honoring boundaries. Always, always the patient must be granted permission to say no. The waiting is instructive. It reminds everyone that reconciliation is an invitation.

Here is a secret. Little words come in stories. In my hospital work our stories find each other. My story, the patient's story, God's story—somehow these come together. The stories are recombined in ways that create something new and beautiful. No one can see it coming. Everyone is changed.

A thirty-six-year-old man had an unexpected heart attack. He was fit and athletic. Now his entire body was consumed with the aftermath of bypass surgery. He was the same age as my cousin who died of a heart attack. You never lead with your own story, especially on such a sensitive issue. But with time our stories discovered each other. I spent hours with this patient and his parents. They were faintly Episcopal but hadn't been to church in ages. Everyone had questions about what had happened, why, and what the future would hold.

I don't typically wear necklaces. On that day I was wearing a leatherback sea turtle pendant. Coincidentally it had belonged to my cousin. It was made of silver and had intricate designs on its back, like the real thing. The young man was smitten. He wanted to know everything about it. Where did it come from? Why did my cousin like it? Was it spiritually meaningful? He was struggling to find reconciliation with his new reality–in the very prime of life, he had crashed headlong into mortality.

I told a story. The turtle was my cousin's favorite animal from childhood, a representation of his identity. He admired the slow wisdom of sea turtles. They often lived longer than humans. Awkward on land, they became elegant and agile in deep water. Sea turtles, especially leatherbacks, were capable of diving to tremendous depths, many thousands of feet down. My cousin loved that leatherbacks were cosmopolitan citizens who could be found in every ocean on Earth. The turtle was a reminder of God's infinite creativity. Wearing the pendant kept my cousin's story close to my own.

Two days later I returned to visit the patient. The hospital room was unrecognizable. There were helium balloons and signs and get-well stuff everywhere. Everything featured turtles. There were turtle slippers on the floor. On the bathroom door was a long, blue turtle robe. A giant, stuffed leatherback turtle sat in the chair next to his bed. The patient was sheepish. He told me his mother had gone overboard. But it was clear. The turtle was his animal. For the first time he referenced God, who must be great and wonderful to design such a beautiful creature. Perhaps God had designed him too.

A year later I heard from the patient. He was taking a trip with his family to Florida. He had learned the leatherbacks returned each year to have their young on protected beaches. Would I be willing to come? Would I baptize him on that beach? He had already obtained a permit from the state department of wildlife. He had a letter of affirmation from his pastor. Everything was ready.

I went and it was life changing. We did the baptism at sundown. The patient's extended family was present. It was one of those wonderful tropical evenings where the clouds were turning colors, from orange to pink to mauve to purple. I read scripture and talked about how baptism is a reconciling act, a sacramental embrace from the God who seeks restored relationship with us.

They emerged from the dry sand right after the patient came up from the water. There were three of them. They were small, no more than a few inches long, with strong flippers which left tracks on the beach. They were leatherback turtle hatchlings headed for the ocean. We watched them silently with awe. At times the baby turtles struggled mightily. But always they moved toward the water. They too were coming for baptism.

A child in the group broke the silence. In a small voice he named the hatchlings. The first was Faith. The second was Hope. The last was Love. The turtles entered the water and disappeared beneath the waves. Each leatherback was a little word made bigger by the moment. The words anchored a new story. In the story we are named, sealed through baptism, and reconciled with the God of infinite concern.